YOU SUCK AT PIANO

A PIANO METHOD FOR ADULTS

Dr. Joel Pierson

Richard—
You Stink!

Joel

MASCOT® BOOKS

FORWARD

Fact! Learning to play the piano is more complicated than learning to fly a spaceship. According to NASA, a professional astronaut needs to have a bachelor's degree in science, 20/20 vision, good blood pressure, and 1,000 hours of pilot-in-command time in a jet aircraft. That's nothing. A pianist starts taking lessons around age 5 and practices for hours a day for 15-20 years before he or she can make any money at it. Let's average 2 hours of practice a day (less when you are young, much more when you are older) for 20 years. That's about 15,000 hours of practicing—all while paying people good money to criticize you.

Now it's my turn! No, I can't be there in person to give you the criticism you deserve; sorry, I'm just one person. So take this book. It's the culmination of years of hard work and faithful testing of my teaching methods on hundreds of students. Actually no, I just hate the other books, which are stupid, and always consist of random, terrible pieces of music with dumb titles. There's so much great music that's available to play, I could never waste anyone's time with that crap. Even little kids want to play Für Elise. They can't, because they are terrible, but they want to....

You won't get to play Für Elise in this book, however. Why? Because you suck at piano. You're just not good enough. Sure, you took some piano lessons as a kid. And lots of adults told you to never stop playing, but you did anyway. And you know why? Because you suck at piano!

My untried and generally untrue methods will surely make you better. Yeah, right! You can always fall back on a career as an astronaut.

This book is dedicated to my girlfriend,
whose terrible, terrible piano playing
inspired me to make fun of her all the time.

TABLE OF CONTENTS

A NOTE ABOUT THE MUSIC IN THIS BOOK

By now you've probably leafed through this book and thought: "Hey, where's all the NEW music?" Well, due to copyright restrictions, I can only include music written before 1920-something. So, no top 40 for you! The good news, if you can handle it, is that most of the popular music today is bad (could this be related to why YOU are so bad?) but there's a lot of wonderful music written before 1920-something.

I should also point out that I have adapted and arranged pretty much ALL of these pieces. They have been simplified, transposed, edited, and generally mangled... all to try and make them more manageable to play. By doing so I risk the ire of fuddy-duddy classical musicians, which I will gladly risk for your sake. So please don't let my work be for naught.

And now, for no reason, here's a trash panda riding a boatercycle.

HIGH PRAISE FROM SOMEONE WHO THINKS HE'S FAMOUS

When you look at a piano, what do you see? Is it the endless possibilities contained therein—symphonies unwritten, melodies undiscovered, chords not yet dreamed by humankind? Or are you more practical, perhaps viewing the instrument as merely a collection of keys, some black, some white? Or do you experience something else entirely, something inexplicable, dark, and unsettling?

No matter what your answer may be, I bring you good news. This book, written by my close personal friend Jake Paulson, will change you—forever. It will mold your tender, clumsy hands, so used to awkwardly grasping at dissonance, into those of a top-tier musical artisan. After reading through this treatise even once, you will become, in the eyes of the brother/sisterhood of professional musicians, no longer an embarrassing joke, but rather, a colleague.

This book changed my life, and I can say without risk of overstatement that it will also change yours. I wish you well on your journey, and should you ever see me backstage after one of my many sold-out arena shows, please accept my full permission to give me the knowing glance of a professional pianist, secure in the knowledge that it will—nay, must—be returned.

Bon chance!

Dr. Brian Wecht, Ph.D.
Professional Musician, *Ninja Sex Party*

CHAPTER 0

FUNDAMENTALS

YOU'RE IN OVER YOUR HEAD

Hey, dummy! Here's a drawing of a piano keyboard and a grand staff—two sets of horizontal lines (also called staves) where the notes are positioned. The right hand usually plays the higher pitches (also referred to as notes), which are found next to the "treble clef" (looks like a wizard's staff got into a fight with the letter "S"). The left hand usually plays the pitches next to the "bass clef" (looks like a sperm chasing its tail), but not always— so you're screwed!

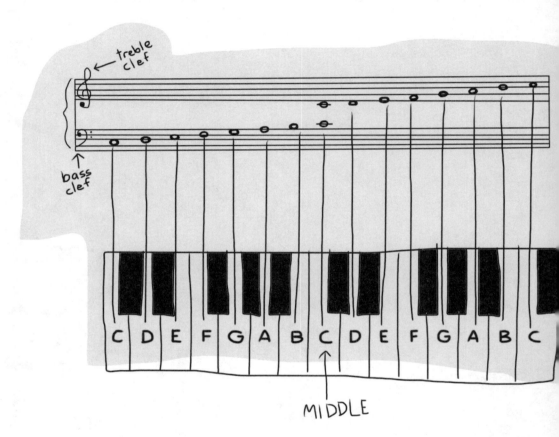

The two clefs are not the same! Look at middle C. It's on an extra line below the staff in the treble clef, but it also exists on an extra line above the staff in the bass clef. Isn't that confusing? It's the same freaking pitch! And it's not even on one of the regular lines!

While we're at it, there are only seven pitches (A-G), and they cycle over and over from the bottom of the piano to the top. When you sit at the piano, dead center, middle C points directly at the worst pianist in the room (that's you).

WHERE ARE THOSE DANG PESKY NOTES?

Without the treble clef and bass clef telling you where the pitches are, you would be even more pathetic and helpless. Learn acronyms to remember where the pitches are found. Here are the ones I teach children on their first day of piano lessons. Hopefully you can follow along.

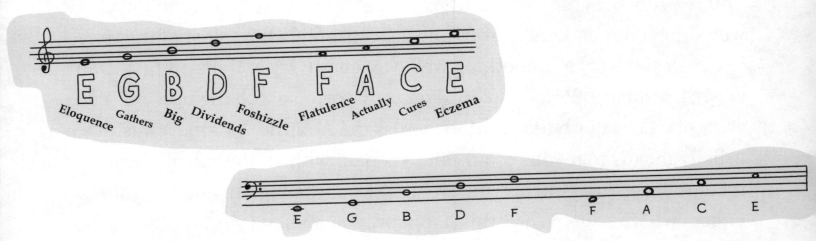

COUNTING TO FIVE HAS NEVER BEEN MORE DIFFICULT

Throughout this book you'll see little numbers above and below the notes. This is to help your little pea-brain coordinate the correct fingers with the correct notes.

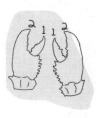
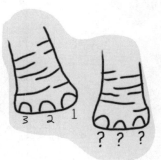
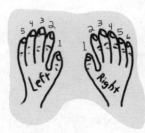

PRACTICE MAKES POO-FECT

Here are a few tips to turn your fruitless attempts at practicing into slightly less fruitless attempts at practicing.

Play Everything Painfully Slow

You're probably going to sound painful at any speed, so you might as well drag it out and make everyone else miserable too. Most of the time, in our desire to play something well, we tend to try and play it fast. Don't be such a square! Practice slow. You are a tortoise walking upwind. You are a plastic water bottle floating across the Atlantic. Making a mistake usually means that your brain can't keep up with all the calculations it takes to read the music, comprehend what's going on, and tell your fingers where to go. When this happens, you must go slower. This is the only way to get better. You'll play Für Elise yet!*

Play Everything Hands Separate at First

That means one hand at a time, you simpleton! Using two hands requires processing twice as much information. Never try to play a piece for the first time with both hands. You can't do it. Trust me, TRUST ME, you can't. Frustration at practicing comes from not being able to keep up—so play slow, and play hands separately. You need to have realistic expectations in order to stave off frustration.

*No, you won't.

Count

Your sense of rhythm is probably terrible. You need to count the beats. Constantly. In your head, out loud, whatever. Write the numbers on the sheet music. Just don't show any "real" musicians what you did or they will laugh at you, because musicians are very mean people.

Where to Put Your Hands

With every piece, you need to know where to put your hands. The fingering can be a clue. If there's a little "1" above the first note, you know that's where to put your thumb—if you can find it! If there is no obvious fingering, look for the lowest or highest pitch, and put your thumb or pinky finger on that pitch. (Right hand: thumb for lowest, pinky for highest. The opposite goes for your left hand. Duh.) As you get to know each piece, you may want to write in your own fingerings to help you remember.

There's No Substitute for a Good Teacher

As amazing as this book surely is, any new piano student should get a few lessons (minimum) from a qualified teacher. Going from zero piano skills to crappy piano skills is hard, as you will soon see, and a teacher will help.

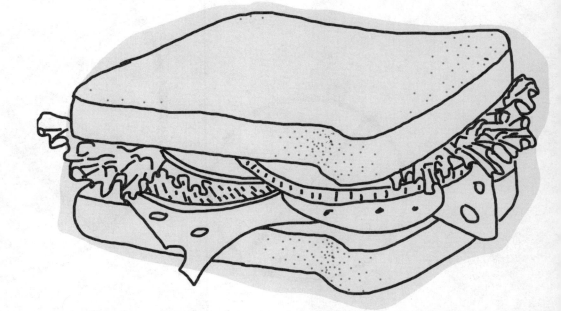

Bring your new piano teacher a sandwich.

YOUR AWKWARD HANDS

Do your hands look super awkward when you try to play the piano? Does your posture remind you of Quasimodo? Is your left hand particularly useless? Here are some tips to improve your playing technique.

Hang your hands at your sides. Totally relaxed. Shake them for a few seconds. Relax again.

Now look at your hands. Do you see how the fingers naturally curve? Like you are cupping a ball? That's EXACTLY what they should look like when they rest on the piano keys.

Move your hands, one at a time, to the piano, all the while focusing on keeping the exact by-your-side relaxed shape. Now, pretend you are cupping your tiny dinosaur butt-brain between your palm and the piano keys. Practice doing this until it feels natural.

FINAL HAIL MARY ADVICE

Don't let your fingers flatten when you play. Each knuckle should be curved. Don't let them "pop" the other direction.

You'll need a lot of practice to play "relaxed." One common problem with sucky piano players is their ring or index fingers jumping off the keys when they play. This "Elton John drinking tea" position is really bad for learning to play the piano.

Try tying your right hand behind your back for a day. Then tape your left thumb to your hand. This won't help your piano playing much, but it will show you what it's like to be one-handed and without opposable thumbs.

Ready to get started? I'm glad I don't have to listen to it!

CHAPTER 1
THE BASICS

BUTCHER YOUR FIRST SONG!

Let's start nice and easy (for me, anyway). Consult the keyboard chart to find the notes. Consult the fingering chart if you forget how to count to five. Check out all the "New Crap" that you have to learn in order to play this piece:

Time Signature

The numbers 4/4 are called a time signature. The upper 4 indicates that there are 4 beats per measure. The lower 4 indicates that a quarter note should be considered 1 beat. What's a beat, you say? Oh my. Think of a ticking clock. Every tick is a beat, never stopping, steadily inching toward your inevitable doom.

Measure

Also referred to as a "bar," this is the space between the vertical lines which contain the notes. Each measure, unless otherwise indicated, contains the same number of beats.

Barline

The vertical lines which separate the music into measures. After every barline, start counting at "1" again.

Quarter Note

The black note with a stem. In this piece, a quarter note gets 1 beat of time.

Half Note

The white note with a stem. A half note typically gets 2 beats of time.

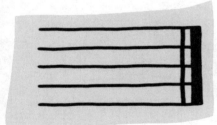

Double Barline

Indicates the end of the piece.

Seem complicated? Remember, Beethoven was almost completely deaf when he wrote his 9th Symphony. He laughs at you from the grave.

LUDWIG VAN BEETHOVEN

Ludwig van Beethoven was a bad ass. Unlike you. You are more of a sad ass.

Beethoven was deaf. If he were alive today, he'd be more than happy to stay deaf if it meant he didn't have to listen to your rendition of "Ode to Joy." Speaking of which, this famous melody (which you are about to murder) is actually a drinking song he heard before he lost his hearing. He was able to turn a common beer-hall song into an artistic pillar of Western Civilization. But, hey, congratulations on finally discovering where you left your car keys last week.

ODE TO JOY

Trad. German, adapted by
Ludwig van Beethoven in 1824

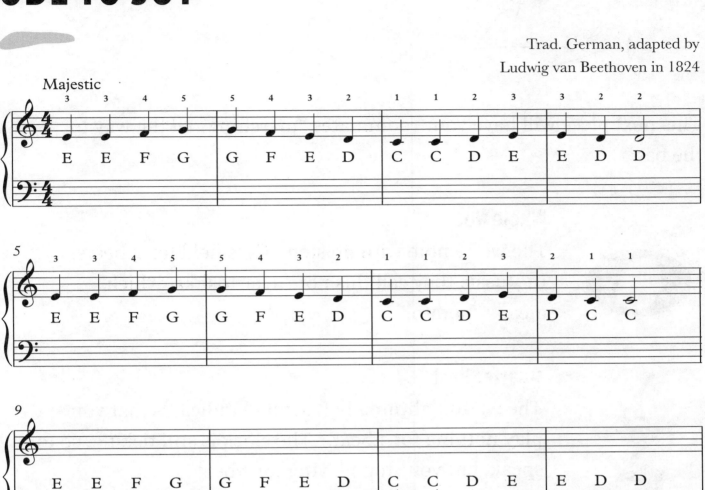

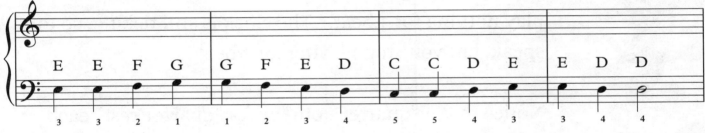

Composer Fun Fact! Beethoven took the legs off four pianos in his apartment so he could feel the vibrations on the floor. He also terrorized his nephew. Look it up.

21

This next piece will have your roommates "marching" all the way to the bar!

Whole Note

The white note with no stem. Gets held for 4 beats. In Russia they call this note a kartoshka, which means "potato."

Quarter Rest

The weird lightning bolt symbol indicates that you play nothing for 1 beat.* The clock is still ticking, so to speak, but you stop playing for 1 beat.

Notice that a "quarter note" and a "quarter rest" each get 1 beat of time, not a quarter of a beat of time. Why is this? Since most music is in 4/4, a "quarter note" is equal to a quarter of a measure. Thus, 1 beat. This is not as clear as it should be, and I don't blame you for not fully understanding it.

*Personally, I'd prefer it if you played nothing forever.

WHEN THE SAINTS GO MARCHING IN

Trad. American

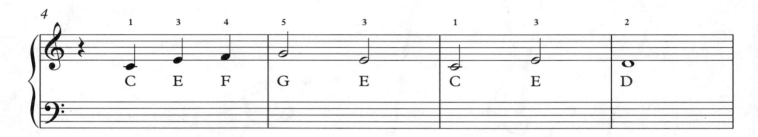

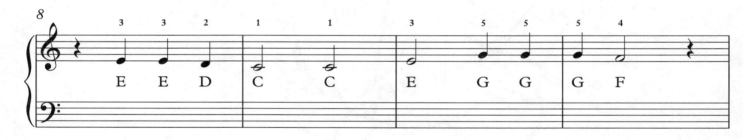

Now let's try it with the left hand!

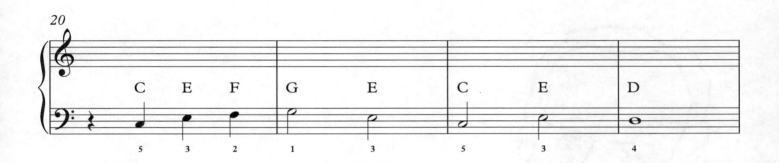

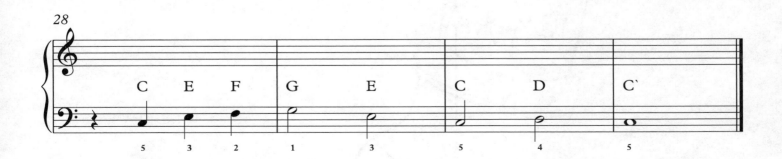

PETER ILYICH TCHAIKOVSKY

Peter Ilyich Tchaikovsky did really well for himself, considering he lived in Russia. In the ways of love, however, not so much. Secretly gay, his marriage lasted only six weeks before he started having serious anxiety about sharing a bed with a woman. I have that too, apparently, and I'm straight! Tchaikovsky wrote a lot of highly praised ballet music, as this was a good way to see male dancers swish about on stage.

Ledger Lines

A ledger line is added above or below a staff in order to make room for more notes on the staff. Just when you think you kind of know where middle C is...

Half Rest

A rectangle which indicates 2 beats of rest. The half rest lies above the middle line of the staff, as if it still has some hope that you will get better.

Whole Rest

The whole rest (4 beats) lies below the middle line of the staff, as if it is drowning itself in misery after hearing you practice.

System

A system of music is one horizontal grand staff. Most pieces in this book have four systems per page. Swan Lake sure does!

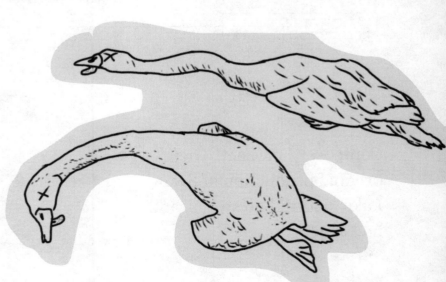

These swans are dead.
Your maleficent piano
playing killed them.

SWAN LAKE

Peter Ilyich Tchaikovsky
written in 1876

Composer Fun Fact! The original production of Swan Lake featured no swans, and no lakes!

Eighth Notes

An eighth note is a black note that appears by itself with a flag or "beamed" together in a group of twos or fours. An eighth note gets 1/2 of a beat of time. Two eighth notes beamed together equals 1 beat.

Eighth Rest

The other weird-looking symbol you haven't seen yet. An eighth rest indicates 1/2 of a beat of rest. One eighth note + one eighth rest equals 1 beat. And yes, I know it's called an eighth rest but it looks like a 7.

Counting with "Ands"

Hot tip! When dealing with eighth notes, count "1 and 2 and 3 and 4 and." Note that numbers meant to help you count appear between the two staves and are larger than the fingering numbers (which are typically found above or below the grand staff).

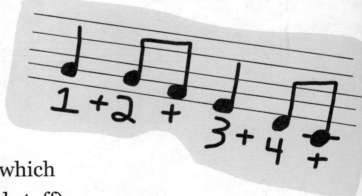

SIMPLE GIFTS

Trad. American

Slow

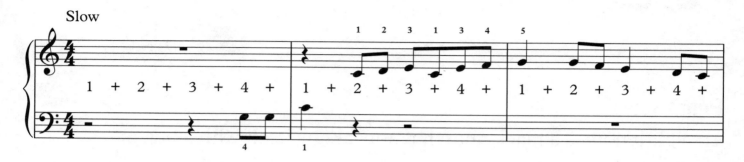

RHYTHM CHART

Let's take a second to review all of the rhythms that we've learned so far!

Note		Rest
♪	Eighth (½ beat)	↸
♩	Quarter (1 beat)	𝄽
♩	Half (2 beats)	▬
♩.	Dotted half* (3 beats)	▬.
𝅝	whole (4 beats)	▬

*Dotted half notes and rests will be introduced later.

Pickup Bar

This piece starts with a measure containing only 1 beat. What??? Didn't I just say that every measure has the same number of beats? Sometimes the first measure in a piece has less than the full number of beats. When this happens, whatever weirdness is in the first measure is subtracted from the end of the piece. So if a piece in 4/4 time has 1 beat in the first bar, the last bar will only have 3 beats! Usually! Sometimes composers say "that's stupid" and don't bother. But I bothered. I bothered very much.

¡Example!

The Star-Spangled Banner starts with a pickup bar of 1 beat. "Spangled"... who came up with that one?!

LOCH LOMOND

Trad. Scottish

Ballad

ANTONÍN DVOŘÁK

Antonín Dvořák was a Czech composer and distant relative of my ex-girlfriend, which made her feel that her musical taste was superior to mine. Well she can feel all she wants. No seriously honey, go ahead and feel. Anyway, Dvořák spent a few years living in America, and was a big fan of the copious amounts of freedom that he found there. He firmly believed that American composers should write music based on the Native- and African-American traditions, and stop piggybacking off of European composers. Almost no one listened.

FROM THE NEW WORLD

Both hands play at the same time!*

Antonín Dvořák
written in 1893

*You're toast!

Composer Fun Fact! Dvořák really
liked trains!

new crap

Here we go again! Throughout this book some pieces are repeated, only in more difficult versions.*

Left Hand Extension

Notice that the thumb of your left hand must extend to one note past where it naturally sits. In this case, you'll need to play both G and A with your thumb (though not at the same time).

*I assure you, this was done solely to stick it to you!

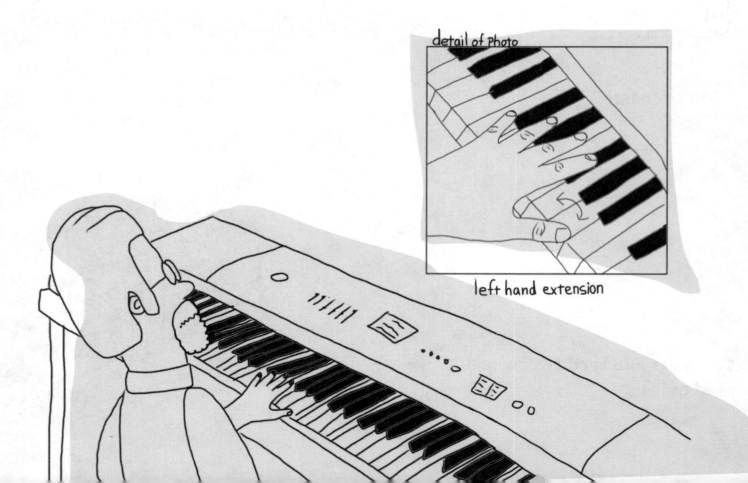

detail of photo

left hand extension

WHEN THE SAINTS GO MARCHING IN

Trad. American

MIXOLOGY WITH MOZART!

Mozart Margarita

If you've seen the movie *Amadeus*, which is 100% totally factually accurate in every way, you'll know that Mozart liked to get down and par-tay. Although the scene got cut from the classic film, he knew how to make a mean margarita. And since you're probably in need of one, I've reprinted it here for you.

Mozart Margarita

2 ounces tequila reposado (any 100% agave tequila reposado will do)
2 ounces fresh lime juice (I said FRESH)
2 squirts of agave syrup (a little less for a more tart taste)
2 oranges (juiced)

Right Hand Extension

In the next piece, starting at bar 13, the fourth finger on your right hand moves to G, which until this point was played by your fifth finger.

2 over 1

In order to combat this change in position, your second finger will have to cross over your thumb in the second-to-last bar of the piece. Gymnastics!

ANTONIO VIVALDI

Antonio Vivaldi was a Baroque composer, which means he wrote a lot of music with extremely uncreative titles, like "Concerto Grosso No. 452." Sounds like a bad Italian pizza. Am I right?

Fortunately for you, the only music of his that your stegosaurus brain will ever encounter is nicknamed "The Four Seasons," which coincidentally is the name of a kick-ass Italian pizza. Vivaldi also wrote Baroque opera, and if you think regular opera is bad, ba-ba-ba-ba-baby you ain't heard nothin' yet.

After his death, his music was lost to the world for 200 years. This is because your ancestors were idiots as well. All in all, Vivaldi wrote around 50 operas and over 500 concerti. Apparently Vivaldi was a big nerd with no social life. Just like you, only with talent. And skill. And motivation. And a cool wig.

SPRING
from The Four Seasons

Antonio Vivaldi
written in 1723

Quickly

Composer Fun Fact! Antonio Vivaldi was nicknamed
"The Red Priest" due to his fiery red hair!

Here's a depressing song for ya!

Watch out—we have a new "thyme" signature!

3/4 Time Signature

Instead of having 4 beats per measure, now there are 3. A quarter note is still considered 1 beat.

Dotted Half Note

Adding a "dot" to a pitch adds half of its original time value. So a dotted half note gets 3 beats of time, instead of 2.

SCARBOROUGH FAIR

Trad. English

ROBERT SCHUMANN

Robert Schumann would have been a real buzzkill to hang out with. His music deals with emotional longing and unfullfilledness.

Schumann had a career as a pianist until he built a machine which stretched his fingers in order to make them stronger. Yes, you guessed it. It ruined his fingers. He turned to composing, where his unfulfilledness might live on to depress people for ages to come. Super duper.

In all seriousness, he wrote some of the best songs in history. My favorite one is "Auf einer Berg" which is about a stone knight who doesn't get invited to a wedding party. Instead, he has to stand there forever, all stone-like and with much unfullfilledness.

To summarize, Schumann was an even more miserable person than you are.

HUMMING SONG

from Album for the Young

Robert Schumann
written in 1848

Composer Fun Fact! I think we've made fun of this
poor schmuck enough!

Oh and look! Another new time signature! I think
you can figure this one out on your own. I said
*think. Not *know.

CHAPTER 2

ACCIDENTALS

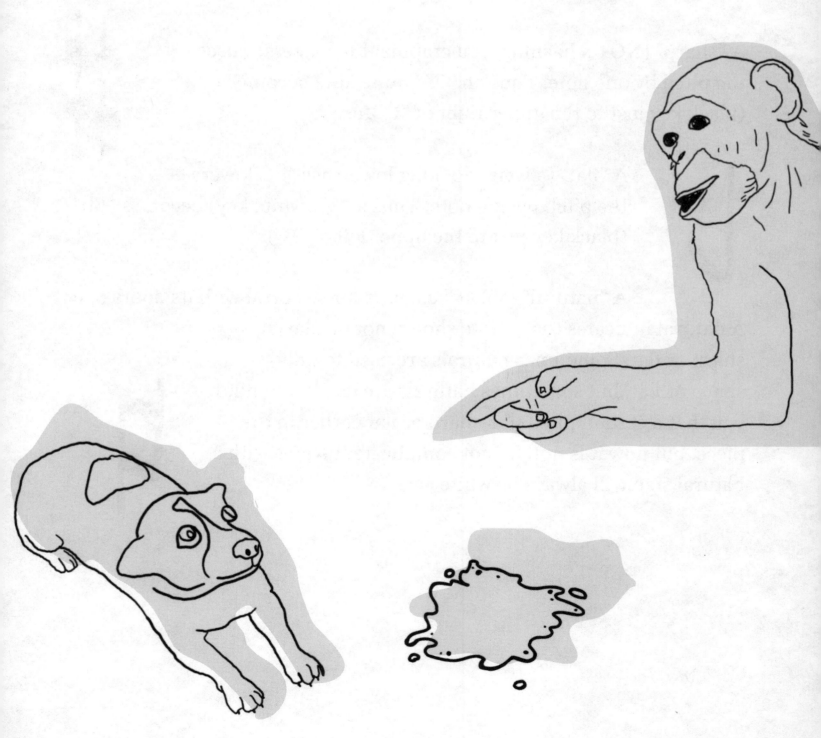

WHAT'S AN ACCIDENTAL?

Notice that so far we have only played white keys. An "accidental" is a little symbol which changes white keys into black keys, or vice versa. As a mentally underachieving pianist, you need all the help you can get, and the three types of accidentals (sharp, flat, and natural), will ultimately help you. For now, though, it's going to be rough.

A "sharp" (NOT a hashtag, you crapulent teenagers) raises the pitch by one note. Thus an "F" (white key) becomes F# (black key just to the upper right of "F").

A "flat" (a weird-looking lowercase "b") lowers the pitch by one note. Thus a "B" (white key) becomes "Bb" (black key just to the upper left of "B").

A "natural" looks like... er, a horse corral with its doors open? A natural indicates that a note should not be played sharp or flat. Sometimes naturals are used to undo a sharp or flat, but sometimes naturals are used to remind you that a certain pitch was sharp or flat earlier in the piece, but now it is not. So not complicated! Notes with a natural sign will always be white keys.

But it don't matter if you're black or white—it's about raising and lowering pitches. What if you "sharp" a B? It becomes B#, which is the same pitch as C! If you "flat" F, it becomes Fb, which is the same pitch as E. You should probably go ahead and quit now.

Accidentals last for the duration of the measure in which they appear. All Fs appearing after an F# in the same measure will be F#s, even though the accidental does not appear again (like in measure 2 of "Egyptian Dance"). Accidentals only last until the next barline, however, which is why in bar 3 there's another # in front of the F.

I'm willing to bet that you will "accidentally" make a ton of mistakes in this chapter.

CAMILLE SAINT-SAËNS

Camille Saint-Saëns may have been French, but don't let that fool you! He wrote a lot of great music, including "The Carnival of the Animals," which is a piece they play for children at posh schools.

Saint-Saëns also wrote a famous symphony that has an organ in it. I'm sure his mother made him do it, because organists are usually sad, lonely people, and they should be able to play in a band, just like everyone else.

EGYPTIAN DANCE
from Samson & Delilah

Camille Saint-Saëns
written in 1877

Moderately

Composer Fun Fact! Saint-Saëns was the first famous composer to write a film score!

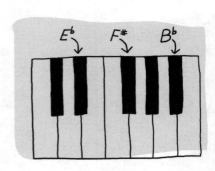

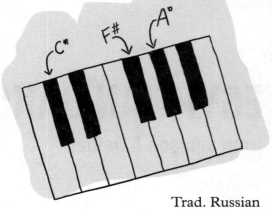

THE VOLGA BOATMAN

Trad. Russian

HOUSE OF THE RISING SUN

Trad. American

EDVARD GRIEG

Edvard Grieg was a short little guy from Norway who composed in a tiny little house on a fjord. There's nothing funny about him; he's one of my favorite composers. You know what—don't even play this next piece. Skip it. You're an insult to his memory.

FOLK MELODY
from Lyric Pieces, Op. 38, No. 2

Take notice, heathen! The natural sign in measure 7 is a cautionary accidental. As we have already learned, and surely remember, the barline resets any sharps or flats, so the C should already be played "natural." Hence, this is a friendly reminder to keep the C natural. It's like the music knows ahead of time that you are going to screw up.

Edvard Grieg
written in 1883

With motion

SPRING
from The Four Seasons

Antonio Vivaldi
written in 1723

Composer Fun Fact! Vivaldi had asthma!

KALINKA

Trad. Russian

VITAS DOWN UNDER

Vitas lived in Sydney, Australia, and could never quite find the time to practice the piano.

A dropbear swooped down from a tree to teach him a lesson.

But it turns out the dropbear was a pretty good piano teacher.

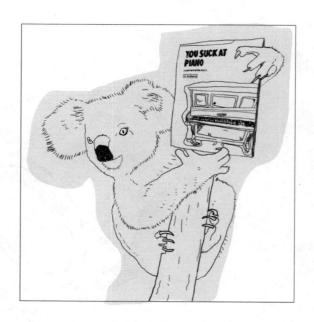

Moral of the story: GET YOURSELF A GOOD TEACHER IN ADDITION TO THIS BOOK!

SIMPLE GIFTS

Yes, I know that you already played this one. But this version is much harder and involves a lot of stretching in the right hand. If you skip it, I will come to your house and make you practice it. I don't want to do that, and I don't think you'd want me to do that. But I don't know you, so maybe you would want me to do that. Whatever—I don't want to come to your house.

Trad. American

COMPOSER COMIC: ROBERT SCHUMANN

Robert Schumann was a brilliant composer living in Germany in the 19th century.

He was composing some of the best music ever written until he contracted syphilis, tinnitus, possibly mercury poisoning, AND became an alcoholic.

His tinnitus left him with a note ringing in his ears. It was an A.

He also heard angels and demons singing to him.

63

The voices in his brain were so devastating to the composer that he threw himself off a bridge into the Rhine, but was rescued by a kindly old boatman.

Schumann spent the rest of his life in an insane asylum, until he died at the age of 46.

Meanwhile, close "friend" of the family Johannes Brahms was so concerned for the Schumann family he moved nearby in order to better "console" Schumann's wife, Clara.

And they lived happily ever after.

HUMMING SONG
from Album For The Young

Schumann is projecting misery and unfulfilledness at you. The left hand part is probably going to ruin whatever confidence you've built up at this point.

Robert Schumann
written in 1848

Not fast

NIKOLAI RIMSKY-KORSAKOV

Nikolai Rimsky-Korsakov was part of a movement to eschew "Western" music and create a uniquely "Russian" style, during a time when various Russian overlords were forcing the peasants to become more European. His music is exotic, like when a Dutchman eats a taco.

Scheherazade is about some guy on a boat or something.

SCHEHERAZADE
Movement II

Did you massacre the pronunciation of the title of this piece? Just imagine how you're going to play it.

Nikolai Rimsky-Korsakov
written in 1888

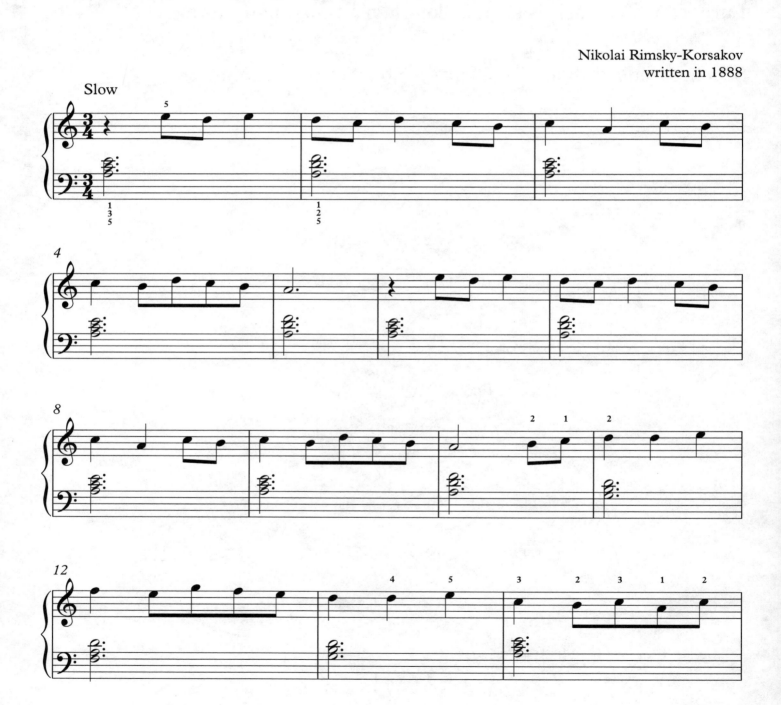

Composer Fun Fact! The best man
at Rimsky-Korsakov's wedding was
Modest Mussorgsky (featured later in
this book). He was drunk at the time.

AUTUMN
from The Four Seasons

Yeah, so there's a lot of Vivaldi in this book. So what? He was brilliant. I'm hoping he rubs off on you.

Antonio Vivaldi
written in 1723

DETAILS

CHAPTER 3

MAKING MUSIC MUSICAL

I may not have heard you play the piano, but I'm pretty sure that subtlety is an area in which you are lacking. Hence the point of this chapter. Making music is about more than just notes. Composers write all kinds of other information into their pieces in order for us to play them correctly. So let's get edjumacated!

Dynamics

Dynamics tell us what volume to play at. The most common dynamics are "p" for piano (which means "soft" in Italian), "mp" (mezzo-piano, or medium-soft), "mf" (mezzo-forte, or loud), and "f" (forte, or loud).

Crescendo / Decrescendo

A crescendo indicates that you should gradually increase volume for the duration of the crescendo. A decrescendo means the opposite.

Crescendo

Decrescendo

Sustain Pedal

The foot pedal furthest to the right is the sustain pedal. Depress the pedal when you see the symbol "Ped.," and lift every time you see the little star. I'm "depressed" just thinking about you trying to coordinate two hands and one foot. Forget about the other pedals—your brain would explode.

There's a lot more coming in this chapter, but since I'm worried about a brain explosion let's start here and introduce more later.

Fun Fact! The real name for the instrument you are playing is piano-forte, or soft-loud, because before the invention of the piano-forte, keyboard instruments could only play one volume (like a harpsichord or an organ). And there's nothing funny about a harpsichord.

FROM THE NEW WORLD

Last time you played this one, it was simplified to the point of unrecognizability. Now it's harder and you're SO totally hosed.

Antonín Dvořák
written in 1893

{NEW CRAP}

Dotted Rhythms

As I mentioned briefly in Chapter 1, adding a "dot" to a note adds half of its rhythmic value. In measure 1 of this piece, the dotted quarter note now gets 1.5 beats instead of 1.

Voices

Look at measure 21 above. See how some notes are stem-up, and some stem-down? These notes are in different voices. This is done so that different notes within the staff can have different rhythmic values. So make sure each note gets its full rhythmic value. Don't lift your finger from the lower voice just because the upper voice moves!

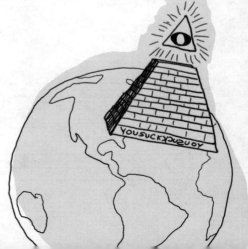

AULD LANG SYNE

Trad. Scottish

Drunkenly

RONALD: A CAUTIONARY PIANO TALE

Ronald hated practicing the piano as a child.

His teacher was a mean old spinster.

Once Ronald had kids he had no time to practice.

But then he found a great teacher (and this book) and everything is groovy!

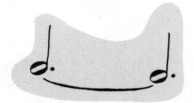

Ties

A tie between notes indicates that you play the note once, but hold it for the combined amount of beats. In bars 1 and 2, the left hand has 2 dotted half notes which are tied together. Thus, you play the notes in the first bar, but hold them for a total of 6 beats. Do not play them again at the top of the second bar!

Fermata

Seen in bars 32 and 51, a fermata indicates that you hold the notes for longer than their written value. How much longer? It's a judgement call. Or a bad judgement call in your case. Snap!

Rallentando / A Tempo

Rallentando (or rall.) indicates that you should gradually slow down for dramatic purposes. A tempo means to go back to the original tempo. Another common translation for "slow down" is Ritardando, but that's just too easy a target.

MORNING MOOD
from Peer Gynt

Edvard Grieg
written in 1867

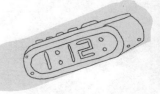

Composer Fun Fact! Did you know that out of all the hot women in Norway, Edvard Grieg chose to marry his first cousin?!

ODE TO JOY
from Symphony No. 9

Trad. German, adapted by
Ludwig van Beethoven in 1824

Majestic

DEATH OF THE COMPOSER

Antonio Vivaldi

Vivaldi, after establishing himself as a successful composer and teacher in Venice, moved to Vienna, which at the time was the music capital of the Europe. He failed miserably, and died in a gutter. No identification was found on his person, and his music was not heard for two centuries.

Staccato

The little dot above or below some of the notes is a staccato mark, and means that you are to play the note as short as possible. Do not confuse the staccato mark with the dotted rhythm mark to the side of the note. I know you will.

Accent

An accent mark looks like a little arrowhead above or below a note, and means that you should play the note louder than the others.

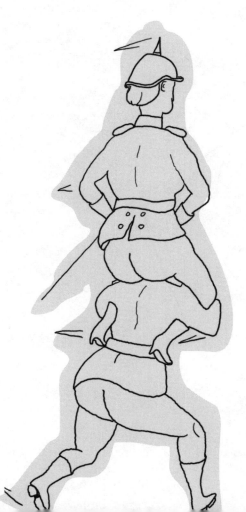

JACQUES OFFENBACH

Opera is one of those things that we're supposed to like, but don't. And that pretty much sums up my feelings about "Jackie O.," as I call him. There's a lot of silliness involved in opera, and Offenbach's operas are some of the silliest. Nietzsche was a fan, though. Makes sense. Nietzsche loved him some lighthearted silliness.

GALOP INFERNAL
from Orpheus in the Underworld

Jacques Offenbach
written in 1858

OPERA PLOTS EXPLAINED: ORPHEUS IN THE UNDERWORLD

Jacques Offenbach was a bit of a dandy. He loved opera, but hated how serious and formal it was. So he decided to poke fun at it. Like I like to do to you too. That was a weird sentence!

In his take on the myth of Orpheus, the two lovers hate each other's guts, and would both rather be "seeing other people." Orpheus is a violin teacher, but Euripides hates the violin, so Orpheus tortures her with endless, terrible violin playing. Hmm... sound familiar?

Pluto loves Euripides, and teams up with Orpheus to kill her, so that he may have her in the Underworld. I forget how she dies.

Orpheus is ecstatic at Euripides' death, and only decides to bring her back from the Underworld due to crushing social pressure.

While in the Underworld, Orpheus learns that Hades is a pretty happening place. All the gods, sick of boring Mount Olympus, come to the Underworld to party and debauch themselves.

Orpheus witnesses the gods doing a ridiculous dance called the "galop infernal," which is sometimes erroneously referred to as the "cancan."

Orpheus reluctantly takes Euripides away, but Jupiter shoots him with a lightning bolt, which somehow enables her to stay, while Orpheus is free to leave. I'm fuzzy on how this shakes out.

This suits everyone's taste, however, so they galop once again. The end.

GEORGE FRIDERIC HANDEL

George Frideric Handel was one groovy dude. He backpacked around Europe before it was popular with college girls and hippies. I think he was German, but he lived and traveled all over Europe (Italy?), eventually settling in London, where he wrote lots of operas (in English for once!). He brought opera to the common people, and made a fortune. He wasn't as good as Bach, but he was definitely better than you.

ALLEGRO
from Water Music

George Frideric Handel
written in 1717

Implied Pedaling

Sometimes pedal markings are only written in part of a piece, or don't appear at all. But that doesn't mean you can't use the pedal anyway. In this piece, you can use the pedal in every bar, then twice a bar where indicated. Pedal use is at your discretion. I already regret telling you that. Too much pedal will sound like a BIG. FAT. MESS.

ALL THE PRETTY LITTLE HORSES

Trad. American

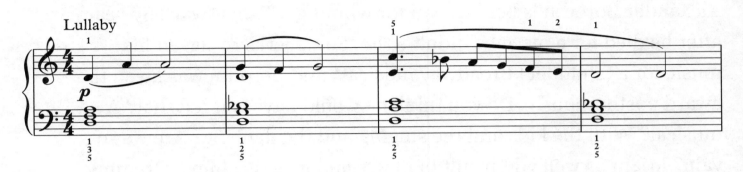

ALEXANDER BORODIN

Alexander Borodin is best known for winning a Tony Award 87 years after he died for a piece he didn't write. Some jerks re-jigged his music for a (shudder) Broadway musical* and Borodin was given the award posthumously. Do you think he would have wanted that? A musical? With the kids and the singing and the dancing? Are we so vain? Might as well add insult to injury and just give him a Grammy while we're at it!

*The musical was *Kismet*.

POLOVETSIAN DANCE
from Prince Igor

Alexander Borodin
written in 1890

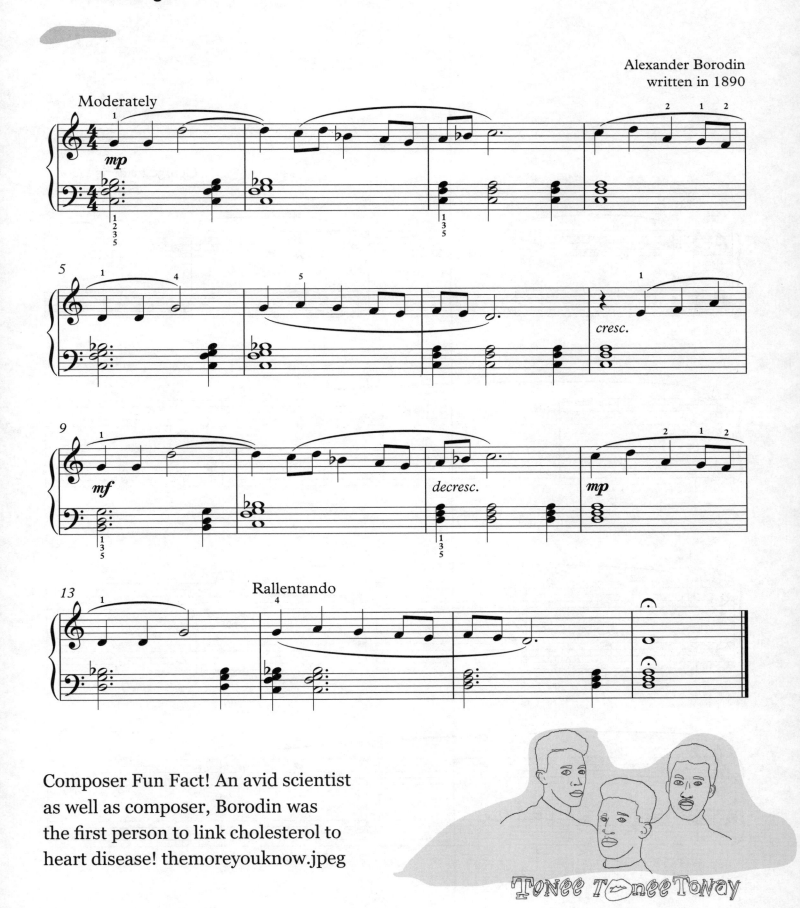

Composer Fun Fact! An avid scientist as well as composer, Borodin was the first person to link cholesterol to heart disease! themoreyouknow.jpeg

AIR
from Water Music

George Frideric Handel
written in 1717

Stately

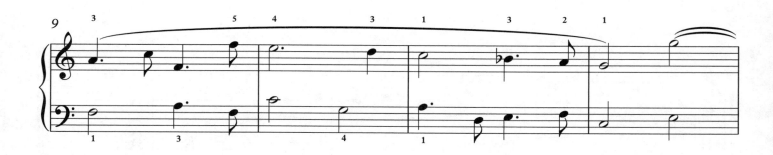

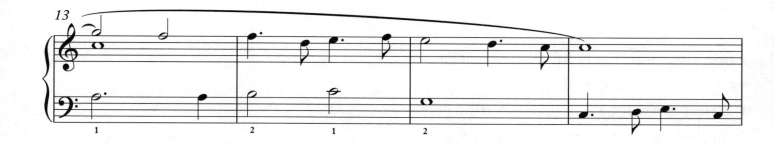

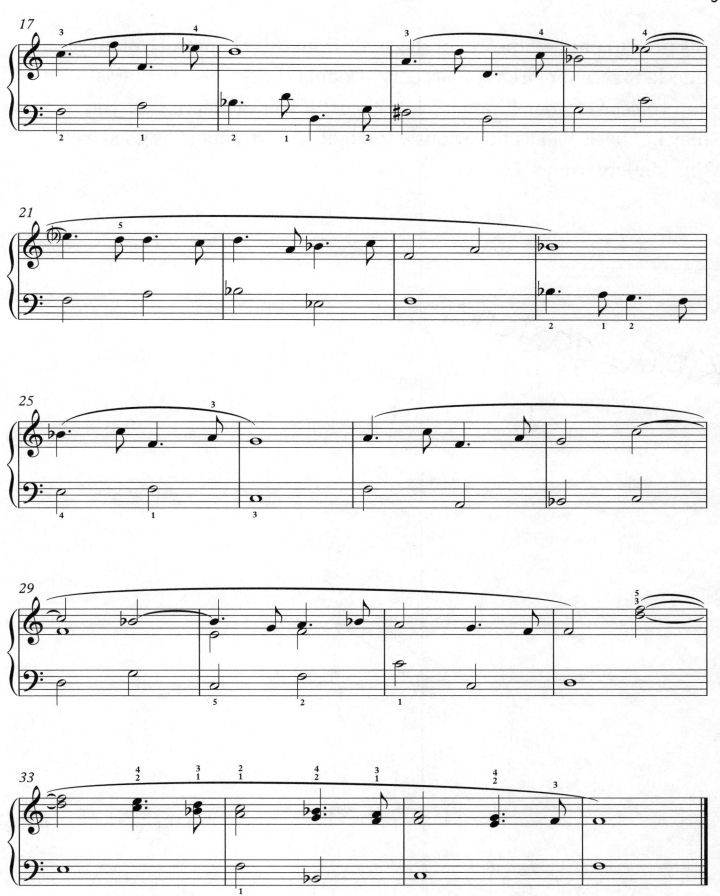

Composer Fun Fact! Handel was lured to London by an
financial offer of 200 pounds a year! Living large!

It's time to put together all of the skills from this chapter. Dynamics? Check. Staccato marks and accents? Double check. Ties, fermatas, and voices? Mother-flipping triple check! If you can learn this, you may not be as bad as I previously thought. You're almost as good as this kindergartener I know.

FIFTH SYMPHONY
Movement I

Ludwig van Beethoven
written in 1808

CHAPTER 4
KEY SIGNATURES

Mr. Brian Bubblegums

WHAT'S A KEY SIGNATURE?

Ever wonder why people always say things like "That piece is in F major" or "It's in A minor?" or "What's that smell?"

Take a look at the next arrangement, "Autumn." See the conspicuous flat sign that lurks at the beginning of every line? A key signature is a set of flats or sharps, appearing on the left hand side of each system, which indicates that certain pitches will be raised or lowered throughout the entire piece. In "Autumn," every B, unless otherwise noted, must be played as a Bb.

Before you give up hope forever, take consolation in the fact that key signatures will ultimately make playing pieces easier. It's a clean, relatively simple way of showing us which pitches will always be sharp or flat.

Another positive: every time you see a piece with one flat in its key signature, that flat will be Bb. You can't have a key signature with a different flat appearing by itself.

Every key signature has two keys associated with it: a major key and a minor key. Pieces with 0 sharps or flats are either in C major or A minor. A key signature of 1 flat indicates either F major or D minor. One sharp is G major or E minor. There's a lot of math behind this, and at this point I'd prefer to spare myself the headache of explaining it all to you.

In this chapter the first three pieces are in F major (1 flat), and the next three are in G major (1 sharp). Then we'll see two pieces in D minor (1 flat), and finally two in E minor (1 sharp).

MIXOLOGY WITH MOZART!

Mozart Mojito

After a trip to Washington state that he never took, Mozart didn't come back with a killer cherry mojito recipe that he definitely does NOT want to share with you. I do so only reluctantly.

1 pound Washington cherries
3 cups ice
1/2 cup fresh mint leaves (pack 'em in!)
1 cup white rum
lime simple syrup (1 cup sugar, 1 cup water, 3 limes juiced and zested)

Put everything in a blender and go to town, Mozart style!

AUTUMN
from The Four Seasons

Antonio Vivald
written in 1723

Spirited

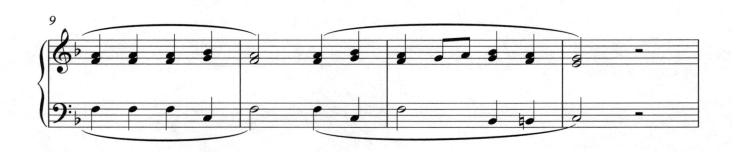

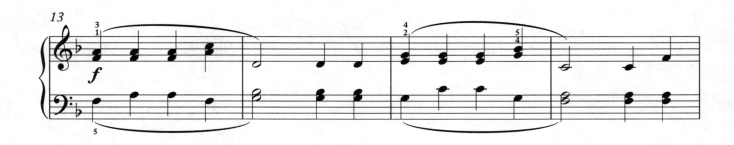

Notice in the first bar of the second line that there is a B natural in the left hand. Here is the key signature at work. The B on beat three in the left hand is actually a Bb due to the key signature. On beat four the composer wanted a B natural, which must be indicated. The next time B appears, it's back to being Bb. Read this paragraph a few times. Hopefully it will sink in.

MODEST MUSSORGSKY

Modest "Mouse" Mussorgsky was going to ride his horsky to the storsky to buy himself some borschtsky. But instead he got drunksky and went berzerksky. The end.

THE GREAT GATE OF KIEV

from Pictures at an Exhibition

Modest Mussorgsky
written in 1874

WINTER
from The Four Seasons

Antonio Vivaldi
written in 1723

Composer Fun Fact! Vivaldi is not around
to defend himself from the wild accusations
I am making in this book.

ERIK SATIE

Erik Satie was first and foremost a composer, not a chair.

Draw something if you don't suck at drawing.

JE TE VEUX

Erik Satie
written in 1902

*"Simile" means to continue. In measure 9 simile is referring to the pedal markings. They will no longer appear, but you should continue to pedal in a similar fashion.

COMPOSER COMIC:
THE ECCENTRICITIES OF ERIK SATIE

Satie was described as "the laziest student in the Paris Conservatory" and "worthless" by his piano teacher.

He refused to take any kind of transportation, and always walked with an umbrella (he detested the sunlight) and a hammer (for defensive purposes).

Some of his favorite foods were coconuts, eggs, shredded bones, fruit mold, turnips, and animal fat. He refused to eat anything that wasn't white.

He also liked cheese, but only of the white variety. He also never spoke while eating, for fear of strangling himself.

Satie did not let anyone inside his apartment for the last 27 years of his life. Inside he kept two pianos, one on top of the other. After his death, his friends found so much clutter in his abode that the stacked pianos were not visible.

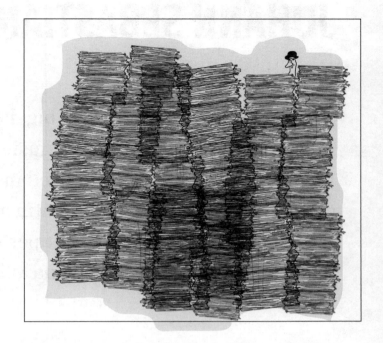

He had also hidden pieces of music in every drawer, nook, and cranny in the apartment, including in all of his clothing.

He only wore identical gray velvet suits, seven of which he purchased on the same day and wore for 30 years.

His pieces had wildly eccentric titles, such as "Desiccated Embryos" and "Flabby Preludes for a Dog." People criticized his music for not having any form; he responded by composing "Three Pieces in the Shape of a Pear."

JOHANN SEBASTIAN BACH

Johann Sebastian Bach is the big daddy of them all. This man wrote (arguably) the greatest music in European history, fathered and raised 20 children, and lived in a dormitory with even MORE children, to whom he taught Latin as a DAY JOB. He was like an RA with a powdered wig and super musical powers. Take that, Isaac Newton, Leonardo da Vinci, and William Shakespeare!

LISTENING SUGGESTIONS: BACH

I'm going to take a break from deriding you to give you some legitimate advice. If you are interested in this Bach character, here are some recordings I suggest you listen to:

The Cello Suites, as recorded by Pablo Casals. An extraordinary set of pieces for solo cello.

The Violin Partitas, as recorded by Itzhak Perlman. An equally extraordinary set of pieces for solo violin.

The Brandenburg Concertos, as recorded by Sir Neville Mariner. Six orchestral pieces to move the hearts of gods and men.

The Goldberg Variations, as recorded by Glenn Gould. Solo piano pieces. Gould recorded two versions, 30 years apart. Both are spectacular. The first is filled with the joys of youth, the second with the reflection of age.

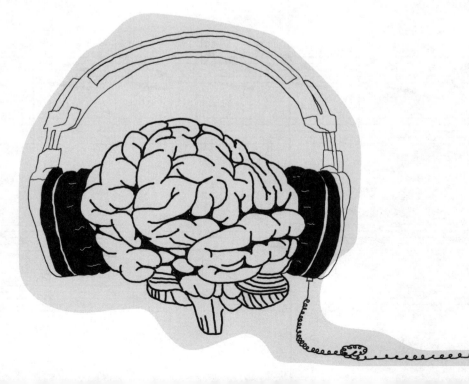

PRELUDE
from Clavier Book for Wilhelm Friedemann Bach

Johann Sebastian Bach
written in 1720

PEDAL TO THE METAL

Piano teachers will tell you that you shouldn't use the sustain pedal when playing Bach. This is said because Bach composed for the harpsichord, which has no sustain pedal. The very earliest pianos were built right at the end of his lifetime, and he never saw one. But here's what I say: since he didn't write for the piano, who cares if you use the pedal? If your shortsighted old lady piano teacher really wants to be authentic, tell her to buy a harpsichord. No? She doesn't want to buy a harpsichord? Ok then. Pedal to your heart's content.

LITTLE PIECE
from Album for the Young

It should be called "Piece for Little Babies"!

Robert Schumann
written in 1848

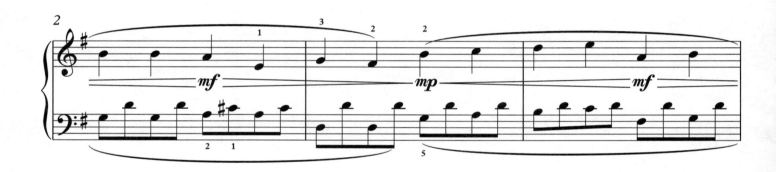

DEATH OF THE COMPOSER

Johann Sebastian Bach

J.S. Bach died from a botched eye surgery. He was survived by his 20 children.

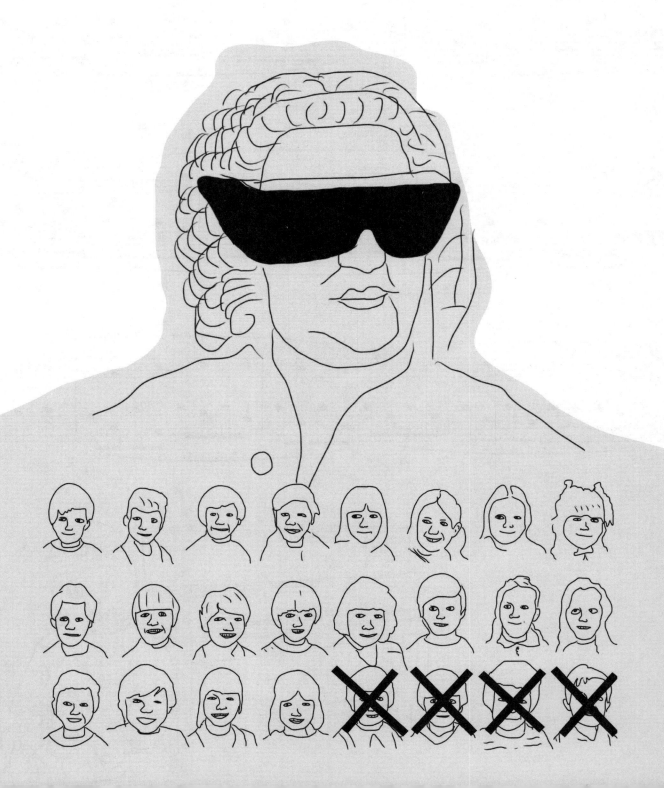

FREDERIC CHOPIN

Ahh, Chopin. His life was brutish and short, full of sadness and sickness. It's better to just not think about it. So let's pretend he lived to the ripe old age of 102, soaking in the sun of Venice Beach, surrounded by loved ones and cheap Mexican food. This is how we shall remember him. It's what he deserved. Longevity, love, health, chilaquiles... he had none of these.

FUNERAL MARCH
from Piano Sonata No. 2

Frederic Chopin
written in 1839

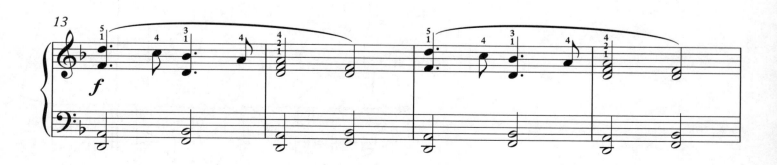

MINUET IN D MINOR
from Notebook for Anna Magdalena Bach

This piece is actually "Minuet in G minor" but I had to change it to
D minor because you can't handle it in G minor.

Johann Sebastian Bach
written in 1725

SOLVEIG'S SONG

from Peer Gynt

Edvard Grieg
written in 1875

FOLK MELODY
from Lyric Pieces, Op. 38, No. 2

Edvard Grieg
written in 1883

CHAPTER 5
CHORDS

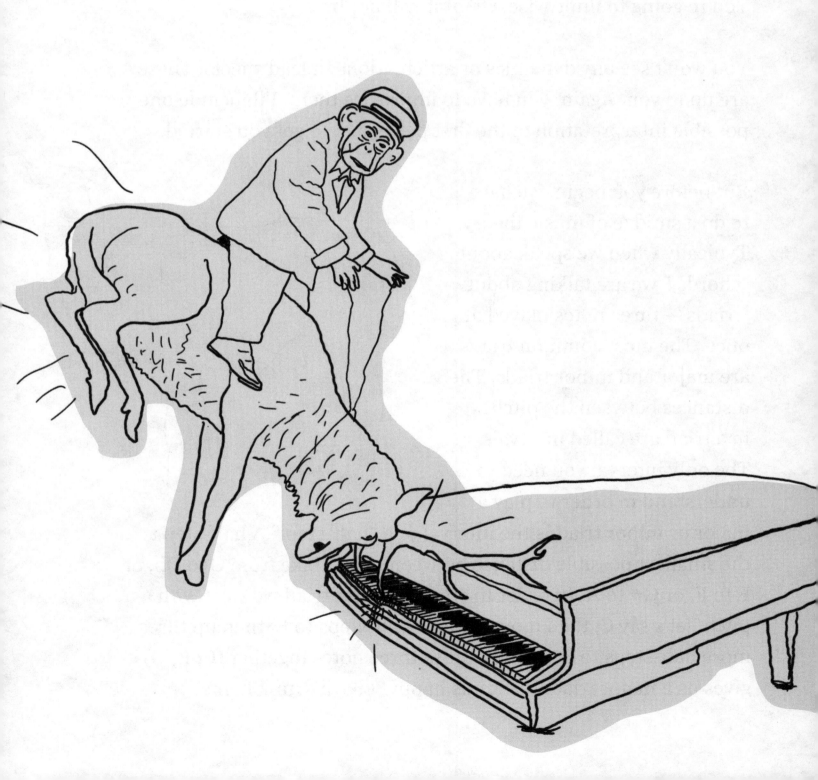

CHORDS

Not everyone plays piano by reading the notes. Many people play "by ear," or by improvising. All the arrangements in this chapter are "lead sheets"—the only thing written out is the melody. You are going to learn and play the correct chords with your left hand. You're going to improvise. Great it will not be.

You won't see any dynamics or articulations in lead sheets. These are up to you. Again, you have to improvise them. I'll include one possible interpretation of the first piece, just to get you started.

But before you begin, we have to do a smidge of music theory. Typically when we speak about "chords," we are talking about "triads"—three notes played at once. The most common triads are major and minor triads. The distances between the pitches in a triad are called intervals. The only interval you need to understand in order to play a major or minor triad is the interval of a "half-step." A half-step is the smallest possible distance between notes. Like from C to Db, or E to F, or G# to A. In order to create a major triad we start with a pitch, let's say C, then move up four half-steps to E, then up three more half-steps to G. Putting those three notes together (C, E, G) gives us a major triad. It sounds happy. Like a drunk llama.

The "cool" thing about music theory is that it applies to every note. If you want to make an F major triad, start on F, go up four half steps (to A), then up three more (to C). F, A, C. Happy llama loves Tijuana!

To create a minor triad, pick your initial pitch (let's use C again). This time, however, we'll move up three half-steps (to Eb), then up four half-steps (to G). C, Eb, G. Minor chords sound sad. Like a morning-after hungover llama that's been painted to look like a zebra while passed out.

In this chapter, the appropriate chord is indicated above the melody. When you see a new chord, play it with your left hand. At the bottom of each page I show you the simplest way to play each chord.

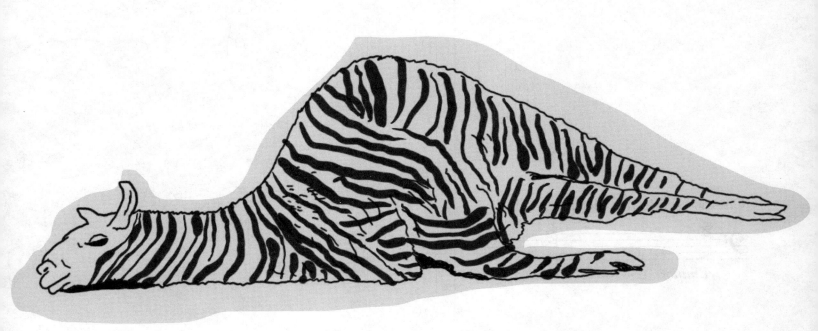

SWAN LAKE

Piotr Ilyich Tchaikovsky
written in 1876

Chords used in this piece:

A minor   *F major*

SWAN LAKE (POSSIBLE REALIZATION)

136

WHEN THE SAINTS GO MARCHING IN

Trad. American

ODE TO JOY

from Symphony No. 9

Trad. German, adapted by
Ludwig van Beethoven in 1824

Chords used in this piece:

G major   *D major*   *C major*

Composer Fun Fact! Beethoven also wrote "Twinkle, Twinkle, Little Star." No, wait.
That was Mozart. I think.

ALL THE PRETTY LITTLE HORSES

Trad. American

MIXOLOGY WITH MOZART!

Mozart Mai Tai

There are literally zero ingredients in a Mai Tai that Mozart would have recognized. But he's just that good, folks.

2 oz dark rum
1 oz fresh lime juice
1 oz Orgeat* syrup
1/2 oz orange Curacao

If you want it sweeter, add a little sugar or simple syrup!

*Orgeat syrup is an almond-based sweetener, and is pronounced "or-zsa." It is very easy to order over the internet, just like how Mozart used to.

STEPHEN FOSTER

Stephen Foster is unsure as to why he is in this book. Sure, he's considered the "Father of American Music" and he wrote some real knee-slappers back in the day ("Oh! Susanna," "Camptown Races"), but come on... he was no Beethoven or Bach. While he was not a "classical" composer, per se, he did live a miserable life, just like the great composers did, dying impoverished at the age of 37.

Most importantly, his music is all public domain, which truly was the biggest consideration

when working on this book. So welcome, Stephen Foster, you magnificent drunk. Also, this drawing is actually of Judge Reinhold, who looks quite a bit like Stephen Foster.

OLD FOLKS AT HOME
(Swanee River)

Stephen Foster
written in 1851

Old-Timey

Chords used in this piece:

F major   *Bb major*   *C major*

142

SCARBOROUGH FAIR

Trad. English

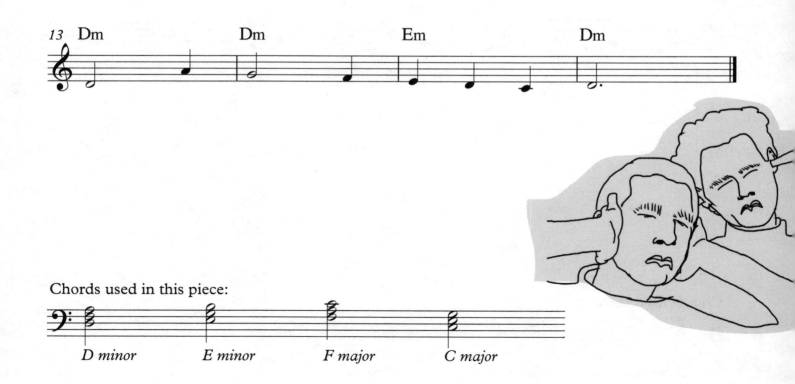

Chords used in this piece:

D minor   E minor   F major   C major

FROM THE NEW WORLD

from Symphony No. 9

Antonín Dvořák
written in 1893

Chords used in this piece:

C major   *F major*   *E major*   *G major*   *A minor*

Composer Fun Fact! This is the last time you will have to play this piece!

144

LOCH LOMOND

Trad. Scottish

Chords used in this piece:

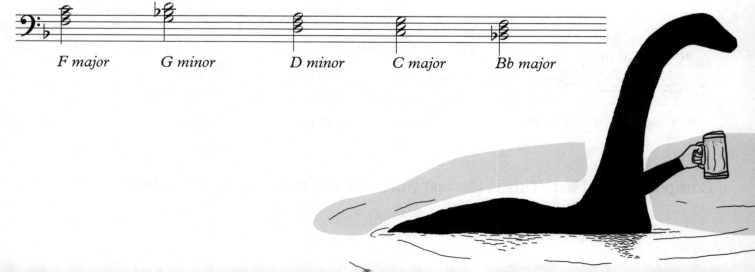

F major   *G minor*   *D minor*   *C major*   *Bb major*

HOUSE OF THE RISING SUN

As recorded by The Animal Crackers

Trad. American

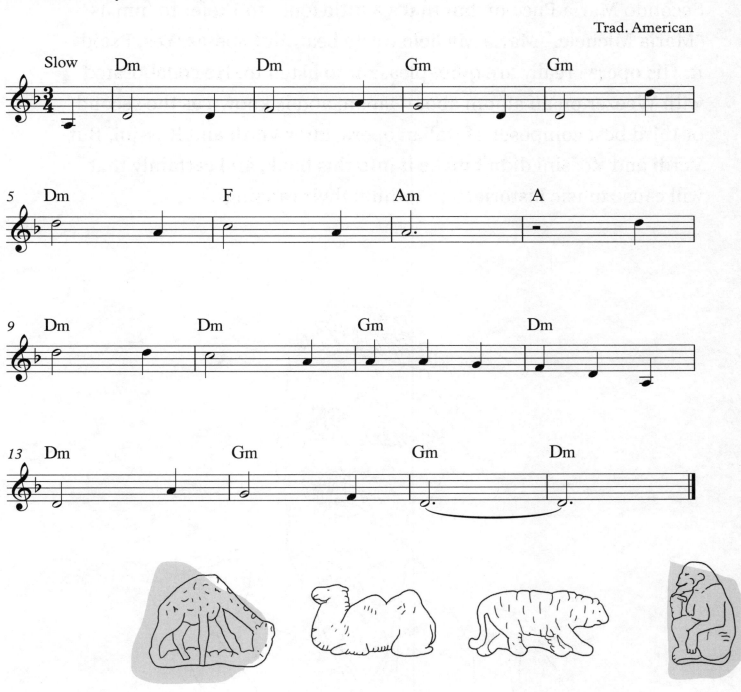

Chords used in this piece:

D minor   G minor   F major   A minor   A major

GIACOMO PUCCINI

Puccini's full name was Giacomo Antonio Domenico Michele Secondo Maria Puccini, but that's a little long, so I refer to him as "Maria Michele." Maria Michele wrote beautiful operas. Yes, I said it. His operas really are quite pleasant to listen to. He collaborated with Weezer on an album about Japan, and is known as the second or third best composer of Italian opera, after Verdi and Rossini. But Verdi and Rossini didn't make it into this book, and certainly that will cause music historians to rethink their rankings.

MUSETTA'S WALTZ
from La Bohème

Giacomo Puccini
written in 1896

Chords used in this piece:

YOU'RE DONE... FOR NOW

Wow, you made it. Or else you turned to the end of the book early, just to peek at how hard the pieces get. Would you have done that to a regular book? Turn to the last page to see how it ends? Well here you go: it ends with you still sucking at piano, but not quite as under-skilled and over-aged as you were before. And for that I salute you, you persevering son-of-a-gun. Like any serious pursuit, learning the piano is difficult, time-consuming, frustrating, and sometimes depressing. You should be glad you had such an encouraging, upbeat teacher as I. So let me leave you with some final advice: thanks for trying, dork.

Certificate of Completion

This is to certify that

Crappy Pianist

Has sort of completed *You Suck at Piano,*
An amazing piano book. Congratulations, you suck
less than before

Date

ABOUT THE AUTHOR

Dr. Joel Pierson has made a career out of music and mockery, or perhaps a mockery of his career in music. Over the last two decades he has worked with artists of great repute, like the New York Philharmonic and the Kronos Quartet, and artists of even greater ill repute, like Linkin Park and Ke$ha. Wayne Newton told Joel he loved him, Paul McCartney gave him a back rub, and Father John Misty played in his high school rock band. He has performed on all seven continents (yes, even Antarctica) and has been featured in the *Wall Street Journal,* the *Chicago Tribune, McSweeney's,* and NPR. Joel currently teaches and performs in the New York City area, most notably with his group The Queen's Cartoonists, a jazz band that plays music from cartoons. He holds a doctorate in music composition with a master's degree in jazz piano.

See and hear more on his website: www.therealjoelpierson.com